IS-144: Telecommunicators Emergency Response Taskforce (TERT) Basic Course

By

Fema

10/31/2013

IS-144 - Telecommunicator Emergency Response Taskforce Training

Table of Contents:

Course Overview

This Telecommunicator Emergency Response Taskforce (TERT) training course is designed to train experienced telecommunicators in one Public Safety Answering Point (PSAP) to assist another temporary, alternate, or permanent PSAP when assistance is needed.

Objectives: At the end of this course, you will be able to:

- Recognize the importance of adequate preparation in deploying to a disaster area.
- Mentally prepare for deployment to a disaster area.
- Physically prepare for deployment to a disaster area.
- Describe the role of interpersonal communication in a disaster area.
- Prepare to work as a telecommunicator in a disaster area.

This course is not designed to replace or substitute your agency's established policies or procedures. Check with your agency, regional, or State directors for specific deployment information and other policy/procedure mandates.

Lesson 1: Introduction

Lesson Overview

The lesson presents information on why adequate telecommunicator preparation is important when being deployed to a disaster area.

APCO/NENA TERT Guidance Document

During the course of organizing a major deployment program for TERT teams, both at the local mutual aid level, as well as out-of state support in large disasters (both natural and man-made), the National Joint TERT Initiative (NJTI) developed a guidance document called the APCO/NENA ANSI Standard For TERT Deployment.

It is highly recommended that every TERT team member become thoroughly familiar with the material contained in this guidance document.

Overview

The importance of adequate telecommunicator preparation for deployment to a disaster cannot be over-emphasized. This lesson contains experiences from telecommunicators who were deployed in the aftermath of hurricanes Charley, Katrina, and Rita. It contains a brief overview of the deployment process as well.

Overview of the Telecommunicator Deployment Process

The TERT deployment process is highly dependent on effective and direct communication between multiple local, State, and Federal agencies.

When a disaster strikes and a Public Safety Answering Point (PSAP) determines outside assistance is necessary, the PSAP will identify the specific needs and make a formal request through established local and State channels. These needs will be coordinated between various States and at the federal level. Telecommunicators in the assisting State will be identified and teams will be created to deploy and assist the requesting PSAP in the disaster area.

During each TERT deployment, a team leader will be designated.

- The team leader is responsible for all team members, as well as all documentation requirements related to deployment.

- The telecommunicators within the team must follow the directives of the team leader and recognize the team leader as the first person in their chain-of-command.
- The establishment of a team leader facilitates efficient and effective communication and management in the disaster area.

Authorization for Deployment

The authorization for telecommunicator deployment must be obtained by the appropriate governmental agency prior to deployment.

Authorization for deployment is not "red-tape"; authorization is a critical component in coordination of resources to a disaster.

Resources from many different States or other organizations may be involved in the deployment effort and each resource (including telecommunicators) must be deployed in the most efficient and effective manner possible.

Each State TERT organization will have a specific, well-defined deployment process, which must be strictly followed. **Self-deployment is not permitted.**
There are several consequences for entering a disaster area without proper authorization:

- Unnecessarily complicating a response effort
- Ineligibility for worker's compensation or financial reimbursement
- Prohibited access to communication centers

Self-deployment can also lead to the draining of already limited resources by a host agency having to accommodate the unanticipated team's arrival and needs.

The level (i.e., local, State, and Federal) and type of authorization may vary considerably among different agencies and States. Therefore, team members are expected to be well versed in their own deployment procedures.

Deployment Outline

The specific deployment process, to include State authority, process, and procedure may vary from State to State.

Please take the time to contact your State TERT representative to locate the specific process used in your state.

As previously mentioned, it is critical to have proper authorization before deployment.

Lesson 2: Mental Preparation for Disaster Deployment

Lesson Overview

This lesson introduces the environmental conditions, the mental challenges associated with these conditions, and various strategies for coping in disaster environments.

Overview

The working environment in a disaster area is generally very different from the working environment familiar to most telecommunicators. While the environment may range considerably depending on the disaster, the amount of destruction, and various other factors, telecommunicators must mentally prepare to thrive and function in less than ideal conditions.

Mental Preparation

The mental preparation for disaster deployment is an integral component of pre-deployment.

The ability to recognize the characteristics of disaster areas and the associated stress typically resulting from working in these areas, as well as different coping strategies, can have a significant impact on a telecommunicator's ability to function in a disaster area.

Disaster Working Conditions

The working conditions in a disaster area may vary depending on:

- The type of disaster.
- The length of time that has passed since the disaster.
- The magnitude of the emergency response effort.

Underlying each of these factors is the dynamic working conditions of a telecommunicator. Adaptability and flexibility are key considerations in working effectively in disaster areas as a telecommunicator.

The fundamental characteristics of working in a medium to large-scale disaster may include any one of the following barriers:

- **Amount of Change:** The recovery process after a disaster will be gradual and continually changing. As a result, telecommunicators may find the "chain-of-command" in response operations has changed, and the process in communicating with responders and the public may also change. Telecommunicators may find themselves in a dynamically changing set of circumstances and must quickly adapt to the protocols that are being followed in the impacted area. That is why it is important that a team leader establishes rapport with agency liaison who can guide team in following proper protocol.

- **Lack of Common Services:** Telecommunicators may find the availability of common services, such as lights, air conditioning, heat, showers, clean clothing, washers/dryers, working cellular telephone towers, and many other services to be limited or nonexistent. Telecommunicators may be unable to regularly contact family members.
- **Sleeping Conditions:** Telecommunicators in a disaster area may have a variety of sleeping accommodations, based upon the available resources in the area. They may sleep on cots and in closets, PODS (trailers equipped with 8 bunk beds and one small bathroom), a church, a tent, or a hotel room without air-conditioning. Sleep periods may also vary and not necessarily be in 8-hour intervals.
- **Working Conditions:** The typical working conditions will often be cramped with several telecommunicators occupying the same and often very crowded area. Other relief and emergency workers may be consolidated in the same building/room, the noise may be excessive from radio traffic and talking, the equipment may give off heat, and the lack of air circulation may make for difficult working environments.
- **High Stress Calls:** Depending on the situation where telecommunications assistance is being provided, there may be calls from the public or first responders and the telecommunicator is limited in sending assistance. For example, telecommunicators received calls in Louisiana from people/family members who became trapped when the roof or their business, church, or home collapsed on them when they returned to survey the damage several days later.
- **Mass Casualty Incidents:** The number of injured and dead in the wake of a major disaster may be staggering. The injured and dead may be unidentified, emotional callers may be looking for relatives and makeshift morgues may be created. TERT members may not only be working in situations where the loss of life and property is staggering for the public, but also extremely difficult for the PSAP employees and local emergency workers who have lost their own homes and loved ones. Members must be prepared to deal with the potential emotional issues of their local co-workers.

Coping Skills

This section will review the various coping strategies to reduce the amount of mental stress associated with being deployed in a disaster area. These strategies only touch upon the wide assortment of peer support groups commonly available to telecommunicators before, during, and after deployment.

It is important to remember, stress and fatigue are common. However, stress and fatigue may easily progress to depression and, in some cases post-traumatic stress disorder. The nature of the deployment and the role assumed by the telecommunicator will vary, as will the degree of coping skills necessary to overcome stress and fatigue.

Most everyone is familiar with the signs of stress and fatigue. Try and remember a time when you were tired, overworked/loaded, and were in a situation in where you had little control over your surroundings.

What were the signs and symptoms?

They may have included:

- Irritability.
- Inability to concentrate.
- Mistakes in job performance.
- Forgetfulness.

The specific indicators of stress and how to cope with these stressors may vary considerably depending upon the:

- Nature of the disaster.
- Work environment.
- Job demands.

Stress in disaster situations may include:

- Fear of making a mistake.
- Disgust.
- Feeling overwhelmed.
- Many emotions all at once.

This section will review several different strategies for coping with the stress and fatigue that may accompany deployment in disaster areas.

Coping Skills – Preparation

As previously mentioned, disasters may range from minor to severe and having an awareness of the potential deployment environment, conditions, duties, and constrains can prepare a telecommunicator to more effectively cope in mentally challenging situations.

Other preparation strategies include developing mental strategies in preparing for a diverse and seemingly "substandard" environment.

Being prepared for deployment to a disaster area includes understanding the key differences in:

- **Chain-of-Command:** When telecommunicators are deployed, they generally report to a team leader from their home state, who will act as a liaison between the task force, requesting PSAP, and incident commander. Beyond the team leader, the chain-of-command may vary and change daily.
- **Functioning Environment:** Take a vacation from your normal way of functioning and try to see how you would respond to not being able to take a shower; sleeping on the floor, with noise in the background, and with the lights on; and eating differently, at different times, and with less than enjoyable cuisine. This experience may be a small indication of your reactions and ability to function in a disaster environment.
- **Communication Equipment:** The specific communications equipment used across the nation varies. The hardware in terms of use of microphones or headsets, arrangement of screens, and vintage and manufacturer of consoles, as well as the software programs used to track and monitor emergency workers may vary. If the opportunity presents itself, telecommunicators may want to examine different systems, not to learn how to use them, but to recognize the differences and similarities. Remembering that the functions of the hardware and systems are the same will help you adapt and quickly learn to use different systems.

Coping Skills – Family Communication

The telecommunicator's possible inability to communicate with family members in a disaster area may be a frequent occurrence. As such, telecommunicators must be sure they not only recognize limitations of regular communication, but their family members understand the possible limitations in communication too.

Telecommunicators should talk with their family and explain how the destruction in a disaster area and shift work may impact their ability to call home. Additionally, telecommunicators who have been deployed in a disaster area may not be able to return home immediately and may need to wait for transportation or until the end of the deployment cycle. When the opportunity exists, call loved ones, friends, and family. Their voice, knowledge of events at home (even seemingly insignificant events, such as school activities), and an outlet for your emotions may relieve stress.

Coping Skills – Coping Strategies

Research into the coping strategies used by and found effective by emergency responders has generally focused on law enforcement and fire department responders. Compounding the difficulty in researching coping skills employed by all emergency responders is the very nature of these responders. They have been trained and have typically put their needs secondary to the needs of the citizens they have sworn to protect and help.

Research has found the following strategies have been effective in relieving and preventing stress. When these strategies are fitted together, stress can be alleviated.

- **Exercise:** Walk or engage in some other form of exercise to "de-stress."
- **Nutrition:** Eat at regular intervals and eat healthy to the extent possible.
- **Breaks:** Take adequate breaks with your team and other telecommunicators. The diversion from work and the opportunity to talk with others in a similar situation will help relieve stress.
- **Out of Place, Out of Mind:** Some people deal with stress better alone and by withdrawing from others, while others may need to talk to someone. Others can simply ignore the current situation and dedicate their efforts to helping more.
- **Sleep/Work Schedule:** Maintain these schedules as best as possible. If you are "off" take advantage of the time to rest, exercise, or to otherwise relax.
- **Remember, It Could Be Worse:** Regardless of how bad things may seem, it could always be worse. As a result, this perception may enable you to reduce the stress and to appreciate the situation better.
- **Think About Other Things:** Take a mental vacation and think about non-work-related and pleasant events.
- **Take a Deep Breath and Relax:** Take a deep breath and remember you have the strength, training, and experience to handle the situation. If you act calm, you will start to feel calm.
- **Talk to Others:** Talk to others in your team or from the PSAP. Discuss what has occurred, what is occurring, and what will happen.
- **Avoid Alcohol/Drugs:** These not only jeopardize job performance, but also increase stress after intoxication.
- **Humor:** The use of humor is often a natural expression to relieve stress and to make the best of a situation. However, there may be times when humor is inappropriate.

Coping Skills – Professional and Peer-Assistance

Depending on the nature of the deployment and disaster, the emotional impact of deployment may necessitate professional and/or peer assistance.

While it is beyond the scope of this course to prescribe at what point this should be considered, telecommunicators should seek assistance when the emotional stress interferes with employment, family, or other social events.

Changes in sleep, appetite, relationships, reoccurring dreams, or other indicators of depression may be signs of long-term emotional trauma.

The long-term consequences for failing to seek help, if necessary, can lead to a number of physical and mental illnesses. Unfortunately, professionals (including telecommunicators) are often independent and rarely acknowledge the need for help.

Lesson 3: Physical Preparation for Disaster Deployment

Lesson Overview

This lesson introduces the physical preparation requirements (personal preparation and packing of essential items) for disaster deployment.

Personal Preparation

Telecommunicators must personally assess their mental and physical ability to deploy before committing to being deployed for an extended period of time. This preparation not only ensures their safety, but also ensures the deployment in the disaster area will be uninterrupted and a replacement will not have to be located.

Personal preparation should include a review of:

- **Personal Health** – A disaster area may not have readily available pharmacies and the air quality may be poor. Ensure allergies, medical or physical conditions will not interfere with their job performance. The consequences may involve hospitalization, severe illness, or even death.
- **Child, Elder, or Pet Care** – If necessary, will relatives (including a spouse) be able to adequately care for children, elderly relatives, or pets during your absence? If alternative arrangements cannot be made, deployment may cause unnecessary harm and should not be attempted.
- **Bills, Mail, and Other Services** – Can someone check your mail, pay your bills, and check your home during deployment? Do not assume you will have internet access during deployment. If applicable, schedule electronic payments in advance. Although local law enforcement agencies are different, many agencies generally check the homes of citizens on vacation and business trips. Extra patrol should be requested. If necessary, stop mail service temporarily.
- **Family Explanations** – It will be necessary to thoroughly explain the deployment to family members. They must understand the constraints and work environment, as well as the inability to immediately call home or receive calls. The discussion concerning deployment between a deployed telecommunicator and his/her family is a personal decision that is highly recommended.

Packing for Disaster Deployment

When packing for disaster deployment, do not assume common services will be accessible. While this may seem extreme, a disaster environment may require an extended amount of time to travel to the area. Remember, that the ability to travel, even by car may be limited by fuel shortages or heavy road damage.

Also, depending on when the disaster occurred and when the TERT team arrives to the disaster area, the PSAP may not be physically ready for additional personnel. The amount of luggage permitted during deployment may be restricted. Therefore, pack only what is necessary and what you are capable of carrying (i.e., smaller and soft duffle bags).

As a rule of thumb, pack enough to be self-sustaining for 72 hours. There are essentially two different types of equipment and personal items that must be packed for deployment: general and specific.

General items include:

- **Identification:** Pack at least two forms of identification, such as a state driver's license, state EMA credentials, and local agency identification card.
- **Documentation:** Travel "orders" or other documents detailing deployment status.
- **Prohibited Items:** Generally, weapons or flammable items are prohibited and should not be packed. If in doubt, ask the team leader.

Specific items include:

- **Food:** Pack lightweight food items that are nonperishable and do not require cooking, such as energy bars; meals ready to eat (MREs); Pop-Tarts; canned goods, such as fruit, meat, soups; peanut butter and crackers; and dry cereal or granola.
- **Water:** A 72-hour emergency kit requires a gallon of water per day for each person.
- **Appropriate Clothing:** The type of clothing needed in the disaster area may differ from the telecommunicator's home state. Check current and projected weather conditions. Wear comfortable clothes. In colder climates, it is always best to dress in layers. In warmer climates, it is advisable to wear long sleeve shirts and long pants (i.e., cargo pants provide plenty of useful pockets) to avoid insect bites, etc. Shoes should be worn (i.e., steel toed boots or tennis shoes).
- **Cash:** The ability to use credit/ATM cards may be limited. Pack cash and at least a roll or two of quarters (vending machines).
- **Medications:** Common over-the-counter medications (i.e., acetaminophen or ibuprofen) and, if necessary, a 14-day supply of prescription medications.
- **Personal Hygiene and Essentials:** Again, do not assume any personal hygiene items will be available in the disaster area. Pack sufficient quantities.
- **Miscellaneous Items:** Other items may include a flashlight w/batteries, a can opener, soap, MP3 player, anti-bacterial soap/wipes, sleeping bag, alarm clock, etc.

Lesson 4: Interpersonal Communication Skills

Lesson Overview

This lesson introduces active and effective listening, techniques in comforting emotionally upset persons, and assertive communication techniques.

Communication Challenges

Telecommunicators who are deployed to a disaster area may face resentment from resident telecommunicators. The resentment factor may be challenging and not well understood for the deployed telecommunicator who is often anticipating an accepting and relieved telecommunicator reception. However, telecommunicators must remember many resident telecommunicators may feel an obligation to remain at their "post" until all calls for service have been resolved, may feel the deployed telecommunicator does not know the communication (radio/telephone) system, the surrounding area, or the community well enough to assume the position; or the resident telecommunicator may feel as if he/she is being "replaced" rather than supported. These emotional perceptions are difficult to adequately predict and may not be present in all cases.

Deployed telecommunicators must first recognize these perceptions may exist and they are not "personal," but rather a common reaction in a disaster situation. Patience, understanding, and a non-defensive response are all key techniques that should be employed as necessary. Most importantly, deployed telecommunicators should step back and try to view the situation from the other person's perspective in order to gain a better appreciation of the circumstances.

Three different communication techniques are presented in this section:

1. Effective/active listening
2. Calming emotionally upset persons
3. Assertiveness

These are by no means the only communication techniques available; rather these should be perceived as the minimum strategies a deployed telecommunicator should consider using in disaster areas.

Active and Effective Listening

There is an important difference between "hearing" and "listening." A resident telecommunicator (one permanently assigned to the PSAP) in a disaster area may be stressed, tired, and emotionally drained. They need to know you, as a deployed telecommunicator, are listening; not simply "hearing" them or letting what they are saying go in one ear and out the other ear.

Active listening requires conscious concentration on the verbal and nonverbal communications of the speaker.

Consider the following characteristics of an active and effective listener:

- **Develop a positive attitude** – Develop and maintain a positive attitude concerning the information sent by or being received by the other individual. A person's attitude will either facilitate or block effective communication.
- **Limit unnecessary talking/interruptions** – Refrain from excessive talking. It is difficult to listen if you talking or interrupting the person talking.
- **Remain objective to the message** – Listen to the person and the message completely. Things or events may be conveyed that are difficult to believe (i.e., working 24 hours a day for three days). If the speaker is mentally closed off, effective communication will not occur.
- **Paraphrase and use feedback** – When the speaker has finished talking, paraphrase what was interpreted. Feedback by the listener ensures what was said was interpreted correctly.
- **Do not formulate an instant response** – Avoid creating a response while the person is talking. When this occurs, listening has stopped and important points to the message are likely to be missed.
- **Maintain eye contact with the person** – It has been said that "listening is done with the eyes." A great deal of information may be obtained and credibility gained by looking at a person's eyes. Is the person being deceptive? Is the person maintaining normal eye contact? In many cases the speaker will believe he/she is being listened to if eye contact is maintained.
- **Control emotions and nonverbal communication** – With practice, emotions and nonverbal communication can be controlled.

Comforting Emotionally Upset Persons

A disaster often has an unpredictable emotional impact on telecommunicators, citizens, and other public safety personnel. When an emotionally upset person or telecommunicator is encountered, certain techniques should be used to calm or comfort the person before effective communication and dialogue can take place.

These include:

- **Use available time:** If the situation permits, take as much time as necessary to calm the person before talking.

- **Allow the person to talk:** Allow the person to tell his/her side of the story or to vent feelings. Avoid interrupting the person when he/she is talking.
- **Provide and enable support:** The use of supportive and reinforcing messages acknowledges an understanding of the person's message. Empower the person by describing the outstanding job they have been performing without being patronizing and remind them that you are only there to assist, not to take over.
- **Physical contact:** The use of physical contact (i.e., hand on the person's shoulder) should be non-invasive and non-intimate, as well as light and brief.

Assertive Communication

When a telecommunicator expresses him/herself, assertive communication techniques can enable firm, yet non-aggressive communication to occur. This section will define assertiveness and distinguish it from aggressiveness and submissiveness. Additional information is provided that reviews the composition and delivery of assertive messages.

The behavior of individuals can be described and placed on a continuum of being submissive, assertive, or aggressive. When one person violates the personal space or beliefs of another, the other person typically responds submissively, assertively, or aggressively.

- **Submissive:** A submissive person does not express his/her feelings, thoughts, or impressions and allows others to violate his/her rights.
- **Assertive:** An assertive person expresses his/her thoughts, feelings, and impressions in a direct and appropriate manner, while maintaining the respect of others.
- **Aggressive:** An aggressive person expresses his/her thoughts, feelings, and impressions in a direct and inappropriate manner, while violating the rights and respect of others.

Imagine you are in a movie theater where several people seated behind you are talking and distracting your attention from the movie. Now, consider how a submissive, assertive, or aggressive person would respond verbally.

- **Submissive** – A submissive person would say nothing and suffer in silence.
- **Assertive** – The assertive person would turn around; look directly at the talkers, and say, "Your talking is distracting from my enjoyment of the movie."
- **Aggressive** – An aggressive person would turn around and snarl at them, "Don't you have any respect for others? If you don't shut up immediately, I'll call the manager and have him throw you out of the theater!"

The components of an assertive message and additional techniques of using assertive communication are beyond the scope of this course. However, additional information may be obtained by selecting the link below and reviewing *People Skills* by Robert Bolton, which was the primary reference for this section.

Lesson 5: Telecommunicator Roles in Disaster Environments

Lesson Overview

This lesson outlines the security and personal safety issues, disaster types, and potential telecommunicator challenges in disaster areas.

Factors that Create a Dynamic and Difficult Working Environment

Two separate factors create a dynamic and difficult working environment in disaster areas:

- Changes in equipment
- Procedures and continual change

The operating environment in a disaster area will often be considerably different than what a telecommunicator is generally accustomed. Equipment, software, and facilities will be different.

As time passes, services will be restored and the operating conditions may change for the better or worse. Priorities, command structures, and the routing of citizen calls for services may change daily.

Security and Personal Safety

The personal security and safety of deployed telecommunicators is a critical consideration. The constituency in a disaster area immediately following the event may range from victims, emergency responders, to criminals.

When deployed, consider:

- Learn as much as possible about the deployment/disaster area. The terrain, conditions, and location of important landmarks. Danger areas, such as those not patrolled by law enforcement or known to have environmental risks, should be avoided.
- Do not go out of the PSAP alone. A "buddy system" should be used. This means telecommunicators should travel in pairs.
- Recognize signs and symptoms of stress and fatigue and react accordingly.
- Make sure drinking water is safe. Do not assume tap water is safe. Contamination of public water supplies and private wells after a disaster pose a significant threat

of serious illness days and weeks after a disaster. If there is any uncertainty about the water quality, use only bottled water.
- Always carry identification and possibly health information. You should always carry your identification and deployment documents. If issued an identification card by the requesting agency, wear it at all times. Essential medical information, such as medical conditions, drug and food allergies, prescribed medicines and emergency contacts, should also be carried.
- No sightseeing. Take advantage of "down time" to relax or sleep. Telecommunicators may become injured or lost while sightseeing in unfamiliar areas after a disaster.
- Wear appropriate clothing. Clothing should be selected based on the working environment and weather conditions of the disaster area. Long pants and closed-toe shoes or boots should be worn in all conditions. TERT responders should only wear shirts, jackets, and hats with their team designations or their home agency designation. If these are not available, they should wear clothing without any team designation. Someone responding with TERT should not wear a USAR (urban search and rescue) shirt. Do not wear clothing that may be considered offensive because of language, images, or cut.

Differences in Disaster Type

The type of disaster will have a direct influence on the working conditions. Catastrophic disasters, such as hurricane Katrina, essentially eliminated safe drinking water, electricity, transportation routes, and brought the entire region to a standstill for days and weeks.

Terrorist attacks, such as the World Trade Center attacks, started and ended within a couple of hours, though the recovery took many months and even years.

A tornado may last minutes, yet the destruction may be widespread over a considerable and narrow area.

Depending on the extent of the destruction, the job duties of a telecommunicator and the length of deployment may vary considerably. The important point to remember is the recovery may change from deployment to arrival. As a result, telecommunicators must be able to adapt and change accordingly.

Improvise, Overcome, and Adapt

Since the operating environment will be different, it is imperative that telecommunicators:

- Overcome challenges.
- Improvise as necessary.
- Adapt to the situation.

This may be a continual process. Be prepared to learn quickly and "on the fly."

Make careful observations of how resident telecommunicators function and ask questions as often as necessary.

PSAP/Agency Structure and Protocol

The structure of the PSAP, technology, and the operational protocol are likely to be different and they may change over time as services are restored and additional emergency workers are brought to the area. You must adapt to the structure and protocols in use at the stricken PSAP.

Structure:

- **Chain-of-command:** The chain-of-command may be different and may change daily. The team leader of a deployed telecommunicator is your first point of contact. This will generally not change.
- **Center categorization:** In situations where the dispatch of calls was separated by function (i.e., different dispatch points for police, fire, and/or EMS), calls for services may be routed through a single PSAP or through a single dispatch console.
- **Dispatcher and call taker separation:** In situations where there may have been a clear distinction between call takers and dispatchers, those responsibilities may be combined in a single position. There may not be a distinction between these duties and the level of multi-tasking between different tasks may be higher.

Technology Differences – Equipment

- **The equipment (i.e., CAD, phones, software) will likely be different, not fully functional, improvised, or nonexistent.** Alternative methods of documentation, learning how to use existing equipment, and a general focus on the job should be the main priority. Do not be immediately concerned with "how outdated" the equipment may be or the "inefficiency" of the current system. These issues can be, if necessary, addressed later. The focus needs to be on learning the system to move to a supportive role as soon as possible.
- **Become familiar with equipment and limitations.** Identify the placement of equipment, resources, and information. Ask plenty of questions to ensure you have minimally obtained a basic ability to operate the equipment. The accessibility of local computer records, as well as the caller's information (ANI & ALI and/or Wireless Phase II location information) may not be fully accessible or functional.
- **Consider dynamics and continual change.** The equipment type and shortcomings may change as services are restored. As a result, the "system" of taking calls, dispatching first responders, and documenting activities may change daily.

Protocol

Consider:

- **Policy, codes, and local procedure.** Existing local procedures may not be in place depending on the nature of the disaster. The policy may be similar to the deployed telecommunicator's home policy, but the CAD codes, if used may be different. In addition, it is important to remember that the use of "10 codes" will be dropped in such situations and all radio transmissions will revert o plain English.
- **Prioritization of calls.** How calls are prioritized and the order in which emergency workers are dispatched may vary.
- **Documentation.** Automatic 9-1-1 and CAD documentation of incoming calls and dispatched units may be done manually with a pen/paper or log book.
- **Working with a diverse group of emergency responders.** It is not uncommon to work with a variety of different first responders (perhaps even including public works and private utility company employees). Keep in mind, these emergency responders may be from different states and may not have worked together before. Thus, the use of plain language in communication is critical.
- **Alternative job duties.** Deployed telecommunicators may be asked to do a number of different jobs/functions. These jobs should be appropriate given the situation, if not, remember you are in a disaster area and advise your team leader.

Request for Service/Assistance

The types of calls or requests for service will often be significantly different from those typically handled on a routine daily basis in a communication center. While it is common for telecommunicators to effectively manage high stress calls and periods of high volume, it is not common to continually handle a high volume of high stress calls.

Be careful in making assumptions based on the number of incoming calls. For example, if 200 calls come in one day, some telecommunicators from larger metropolitan areas may perceive this as a low number. However, if only two telecommunicators are taking the calls and dispatching emergency responders, the volume of calls has a new meaning.

Other Issues and Considerations for Deployed Telecommunicators

- **Geographical implications.** It is unlikely a deployed telecommunicator will be familiar with the geographical area in terms of streets, addresses, and other landmarks. By the same token, emergency responder may find it difficult to determine their location due to the destruction of landmarks and in the absence of street signs.

- **Type of service requests.** The PSAP may be the main point of contact for every citizen need, including restoration of utilities, resources, assistance, city/county offices, and any other type of need imaginable.
- **Quality of information.** The quality of information from callers may be poor. The caller may be emotional, angry, impatient, and may not know their physical location. Be prepared for a high volume of high stress calls. Remember, the caller has likely experienced a traumatic situation and their demeanor may be a result of the disaster and not a personal attack.
- **Responding to calls/questions.** Be truthful to callers and avoid promising anything that cannot be delivered. Avoid giving legal advice. The laws and civil statutes in states tend to vary considerably. What is true in one state may be incorrect in another state. Responses concerning similar questions must be consistent. The availability or lack of services/resources should be identified and any changes noted.
- **Inability to respond.** Be prepared to be unable to respond. The unavailability of first responders to provide a timely response may be limited due to limited personnel, impassable roads, or other conditions. There may not be little, if anything you can immediately do for the caller. These and other difficult calls will be very challenging.
- **Emergency responder requests for assistance.** Generally when emergency responders request assistance, backup is immediately sent. However, the resources may not be available in disaster areas. Additionally, emergency responders may make unrealistic requests (that would otherwise be common in non-disaster areas). Be patient.

Lesson 6: Conclusion

Lesson Overview

This lesson provides a brief summary on the topics covered in this training program.

Program Review

The primary purpose of this training program was to provide experienced telecommunicators with an overview of the challenges in disaster deployments. Having an awareness of the challenges, limitations, and preparation strategies was designed to reduce the amount of stress a telecommunicator may experience prior to deployment.

The nature of a disaster will ultimately influence many of the awareness principles presented in this program. As a result, the only constant, ironically, is change and adaptability. Deployed telecommunicators must remember they are being deployed to assist other telecommunicators in need and the environment is unlikely to be pleasant. However, the deployment will not last forever and there may become a time when your PSAP will need the same type of assistance.